MW01291134

# DAMAGED
# GOODS

# DAMAGED
# GOODS

## *The Restoring Power Of The Father's Love*

**FRAGILE**
**HANDLE WITH CARE**

### PASTOR LEWIS L. TUCKER JR.

**Outskirts Press, Inc.**
**Denver, Colorado**

The opinions expressed in this manuscript are solely the opinions of the author and do not represent the opinions or thoughts of the publisher. The author represents and warrants that s/he either owns or has the legal right to publish all material in this book.

Damaged Goods
The Restoring Power of the Father's Love
All Rights Reserved.
Copyright © 2009 Pastor Lewis L. Tucker Jr.
V2.0

Cover Photo and Interior Photo © 2009 JupiterImages Corporation. All rights reserved - used with permission.

This book may not be reproduced, transmitted, or stored in whole or in part by any means, including graphic, electronic, or mechanical without the express written consent of the publisher except in the case of brief quotations embodied in critical articles and reviews.

Scripture marked KJV and NKJV are taken from the King James Version of the bible, and from the New King James Version of the bible, Copyright © 1982 by Thomas Nelson, Inc. Used by permission. All Rights Reserved.

Scripture marked NIV taken from the HOLY BIBLE, NEW INTERNATIONAL VERSION, Copyright © 1973, 1978, 1984 by International Bible Society. Used by permission of Zondervan. All Rights Reserved.

Scripture marked NLT taken from the *Holy Bible*, New Living Translation, Copyright © 1996. Used by permission of Tyndale House Publishers, Inc., Wheaton, Illinois 60189 All Rights Reserved

Scripture marked AMP taken from THE AMPLIFIED BIBLE, Copyright © 1954, 1958, 1962, 1964, 1965, 1987 by The Lockman Foundation. All Rights Reserved. Used by permission. (www.Lockman.org)

Outskirts Press, Inc.
http://www.outskirtspress.com

ISBN: 978-1-4327-2872-4

Library of Congress Control Number: 2009927694

Outskirts Press and the "OP" logo are trademarks belonging to Outskirts Press, Inc.

PRINTED IN THE UNITED STATES OF AMERICA

# TABLE OF CONTENTS

**The Introduction**................................................1

*The Most Precious Gift!*


**The Investment**.............................................5

*From Damaged Goods To Priceless Gems!*


**The Damage**.................................................9

*Abuse Is Abuse!*


**The Signs**.....................................................13

*How Will I Know If I've Been Damaged?*


**The Question**...........................................19

*What's Wrong With Me?*


**The Answer**..............................................25

*You Don't Know How Much You're Worth!*


**The Beginning**.......................................37

*How Did I Get Like This?*

**The Quest**................................................45

*Why Can't I Find A Good Man?*


**The Restoration**..........................................65

*There's Nothing Like The Father's Love!*

# THE INTRODUCTION

## THE MOST PRECIOUS GIFT!
*{Fragile! Handle With Care!}*

I remember the first time I heard her sing. I was sitting on the front row at Ebenezer AME Church in Roanoke, Virginia. We were just dating at the time and I thought to myself "God, are you trusting me with that?" It was then that I realized how truly special she was. I had already come to the conclusion that she was the one, although I hadn't told her that yet. But a year or so later when I was standing in front of the church watching her walk down the aisle crying like a baby, it was that image that came back to me. Now everyone who watches our wedding video finds it amusing to see this six-foot three hundred and fifty pound man balling like a little girl. All my friends who knew me as a player, a master of the game, just couldn't believe that I went out like that. But what they didn't know was what God was doing on the inside of me.

1

# DAMAGED GOODS

You see even though I was not in the word, as a matter of fact that day I saw her sing was the first time I had been in church since I was a teenager, and even though I was not exactly living the kind of life that God would have been pleased with, at that moment, standing at the front of that church, He reminded me of what He had shown me a year ago, and He answered me and said, "Yes I'm trusting you with My daughter!" It was at that moment that I realized the gift that God had given me. He had entrusted me to care for His daughter, and that's when I recognized who she really was, and I couldn't help but breakdown, but little did I know that she didn't know who she was. You see I thought because she was so beautiful, so kind, and had the voice of an angel that she just had to be perfect; often times the most precious gifts are the most fragile, and although they may look good on the outside, they can be broken on the inside. But you see God already knew that, and He was preparing my heart to take her on the journey of restoration.

# DEDICATION

So it is to Stephanie, my darling wife, my rib, the one who makes me complete, that I dedicate this book. To my two beautiful daughters, Kyah and Kourtney, may you always know the power of your Fathers' Love, both mine and the Great One who dwells in Heaven. To my natural and spiritual parents, Deacons Lewis and Grace Tucker Sr. and Pastors Boyd and Camillle Bullock Sr. of the Haven of Hope Covenant Church, and to the New Birth Kingdom Church family, thank you for praying for and supporting me during this project. But most of all I'd like to thank my Heavenly Father for His Son Jesus, and allowing the Holy Spirit to work through me to minister to the Body of Christ for His glory and the gifts that He has entrusted to me in His daughters.

# THE INVESTMENT

⤫

## FROM DAMAGED GOODS
## TO PRICELESS GEMS!
### *{One Man's Trash Is Another Man's Treasure}*


You know automobile restoration can be one of the most lucrative businesses in existence. Because you begin with something that someone else has discarded, written off as something of little to no value, and by applying the proper treatment; if you are willing to invest your time, care, and attention to detail; the end result can be something priceless, an object of desire, and the envy of many. It's an amazing concept really; something that starts out in a salvage yard can end up worth millions. You've heard the old saying "One man's trash is another man's treasure". But how is this possible?

Because whoever owned it before underestimated its value, they could not appreciate its potential, and therefore mistreated and eventually discarded it, but the key to being successful in the restoration process is being able to see the value beyond the current condition. You have to look past what you presently see and see its potential; you must be willing to put in the time and effort to undo the damage done by the neglect and mistreatment of the previous owner.

You may be wondering, *"What does all this have to do with the subject of this book?"* Well they actually have a lot in common. You see the majority of women fall into the category that I call *"Damaged Goods"*. Most have been mistreated in some manner or another, and whether they have been physically, verbally, or sexually abused, it leaves them emotionally wounded and mentally scarred. Most often they have been discarded, written off as something of little to no value, by the person who mistreated them because they underestimated their value, and could not appreciate their potential, and they find themselves in the salvage yard of life. Going through self-destructive patterns, going from one bad relationship to another, sexual promiscuity, low self-esteem, even bitterness, but just like with an automobile, this was not what the manufacturer intended when he designed it.

Just like automobile restoration, the restoration of a woman who has been hurt, can be the most rewarding process. You begin with someone that someone else has discarded, written off as something of little to no value, and by applying the proper treatment; if you are willing to invest your time, care, and attention to detail; the end result can be priceless. Trust me I know from experience, as a husband of twelve years to a woman who had been damaged. But through the Love of Christ, He enabled me to help restore her to the most precious gift on earth.

You see, I'm writing this book in an effort to help restore women who have been mistreated, break cycles of mistreatment and abuse, and prevent those who have not been mistreated from making decisions that place them in unhealthy relationships. As a Pastor who has helped restore numerous women, and has been anointed to minister to the broken, and as a man who has done his share of damage in the past, it is my desire never to see another woman, including my two beautiful daughters, suffer because of a man. It is also my prayer, for those women who have been wounded, that as you read this book, you would allow the Holy Spirit to minister to your heart that you may be restored. For my brothers in Christ, I pray that you recognize the true value of the gift God has given us in women, and be willing to make the investment necessary to help restore them.

# THE DAMAGE

༄

## ABUSE IS ABUSE!
### *{No Matter How It Happened, The Results Are the Same}*

N ow I'm sure some of you may be thinking, *"Well Pastor I appreciate your concern, and I'm sure that this book will be a blessing to many women, but I've never been physically, verbally, or sexually abused."* Well that may be true, but that still doesn't mean that you haven't been wounded. You see no matter how it happened the results are the same. Abuse is abuse I don't care how gentile he was with it. Whether he used a lead pipe or wrapped his hand in a towel, as not to leave a bruise, it still hurts just as much. Date rape is no different than conventional rape. Just because he bought you dinner first, doesn't make it any better. Emotional abuse can be just as bad as physical abuse.

See the definition of abuse is any use other than the normal or intended purpose. Many men, including myself, at one time in my life, consider themselves to be players, masters at running game. Well what are they playing with, what game are they running? A woman's emotions were not meant to be toyed with; that was not their purpose. So no matter how nice he was about it, no matter how well he treated you in the process, no matter what kind of understanding you may think you had, you have been a victim of emotional abuse plain and simple. Telling you that he loved you when he really didn't, making you think you could trust him and then finding out that you couldn't, left just as deep if not deeper emotional scars as if he went upside your head. Trust me, he knew what he was doing, taking advantage of the fact that you were seeking the love you never had. So he toyed with your emotions, he led you on making it even harder for you to trust anyone, but at the same time, making your desire to fill that void in your life that much greater. And since you still didn't think you deserved any better, you continued to compromise, by sacrificing your feelings for the sake of not being alone, until one day, as a result of all the emotional abuse, you become so bitter that you punish the one good man that you do get. But daughter it doesn't have to stay that way.

They say in rehab, "The first step to recovery is admitting you have a problem." You see, so many women are in denial about the fact that they have trust issues, and that they have become bitter. As if admitting that you have been affected, by how he mistreated you, somehow makes you weak, but what's weak is the way you ruin any chance at happiness you have because you are unwilling to deal with your trust issues. Now I know what you are thinking, *"Pastor I'm fine."* Yeah, you're fine alright. I believe in your case, fine stands for: **F**inally **I**n **N**eed of **E**motional help. Remember trust is the basis of every good relationship and the only way you will ever be able to trust again is to trust God enough to be honest about your trust issues, let Him know that you are bitter because someone hurt you, and give Him the opportunity to heal you because He loves you too much to allow you to stay damaged.

# THE SIGNS

∽

## HOW WILL I KNOW IF I'VE BEEN DAMAGED?

*{All Scars Aren't Visible}*

J ust like with an automobile, the damage is not always visible, especially if you are a victim of abuse. The reason is because as I told you earlier, as a result of the mistreatment and abuse, you felt unworthy of love. So instead of showing signs like avoiding the people who did not love you, and did not know how to treat you, you pursued them in the hope that you could earn the love you so desperately wanted. Instead of withdrawing and cowering from those who had abused you, (*because the enemy convinced you it was because of something you did*), you go right back to these dangerous relationships hoping to correct your mistakes; hoping you'll learn how to not push that button.

You see, when a woman has been physically abused the enemy will eventually convince her that this is the kind of treatment she deserves; that in some kind of sadistic way this is how her abuser shows his love. At first, you're upset when he beats you, but then he apologizes and does something nice. And just because he tells you he's sorry, the enemy convinces you that it's normal, until finally you begin to make excuses for him. "He was tired, he lost his job, I shouldn't have said that, but he loves me." And if you do find a healthy relationship, you can't appreciate it because it doesn't come with a black eye. You think that's how a man shows he cares about you, by putting his hands on you. And although he was only hitting you, the effects can carry on for generations. Because your daughters will grow up thinking that's the kind of treatment they should expect, and if truth be told, that's why you accepted it, and if you're not careful your sons will grow up thinking that's how they should treat a woman, because of what they saw a man do to you, creating a whole new cycle of violence. So you might want to reconsider, because this is the type of damage that physical abuse can do.

Even sexually, instead of shutting down, you become more promiscuous, because the enemy has convinced you that sex is what defines your worth; that that's the only reason anyone will love you. So you use the very thing that they used to make you feel unworthy of love, to try and earn love. And all this happens until you end up in a truly loving relationship, with someone who gives you love without having to earn it, and all of a sudden you begin to withdraw from someone who would never hurt you, you shut down physically and emotionally from the one who you should open up to.

The number of women who have been sexually molested, abused, or assaulted is alarming. By the age of eighteen one out of three girls will have been sexually abused by someone they love or should be able to trust.₁ But what is even more tragic is the fact that because of the pain and emotional scars associated with it, many of them never deal with what happened to them. And the suppression of such emotional trauma can manifest itself in self-destructive behavior such as depression, promiscuity, or alcohol and drug abuse. And once in a healthy relationship, these repressed memories can result in intimacy issues. Because emotions are just like food, no matter how good the container you store them away in, they will eventually spoil and rot, and the longer you wait to deal with them the more unpleasant they will be. That's why you've got to be honest with yourself and God, so that He can heal you from the damage and you won't continue to suffer and miss out on your chance at happiness.

Now women who have been verbally abused have a tendency to develop low self-esteem, lack of self-confidence, and often times approval addiction because they are constantly trying to avoid conflict. But once in a healthy relationship, because of the damage suffered, they become paranoid and defensive because they are so accustomed to being attacked, that they expect it even if it is unsubstantiated. As a result, communication problems are likely to develop, because they are afraid to voice their opinion, and eventually become resentful when they are not heard. So even though he may not have laid a hand on you, the damage was just as bad.

Now emotional abuse, though less severe, can cause more damage in future relationships than the rest, because it causes you to look at the person you are currently with through the mistakes of the one you were with before. It causes you to walk in unforgivness, and unforgivness turns to resentment, and resentment to bitterness. You see it's the one that causes a woman to say, "Because the last guy cheated on me, you probably will. Because the last guy broke my heart, I can't let you get too close." It was this kind of damage that coined the phrase, "All men are dogs!" because some woman had a man that emotionally dogged her out.

See when you've been emotionally damaged you'll ruin a perfectly good relationship, because you'll no longer trust anyone. You'll begin to accuse and mistreat the one man who has proved himself worthy of trust. You begin to sabotage your own relationship because you begin to look at him through the eyes of the one who hurt you. You try and punish him for another man's mistakes until eventually, you ruin the one good relationship you did have. And it's partly because you would rather know you're going to be unhappy than take a chance and get hurt again, because you have allowed yourself to become bitter. *Well Pastor why is it that the damage doesn't show up until I have a good guy? Why do I always treat him bad?* Well it's because when you're in battle and you get wounded, you don't have time to tend to the wound, because you are too busy fighting; but when the smoke settles and the dust clears, and you realize how badly you've been hurt, you will lash out at anyone who touches you. You'll attack them even if they are trying to help. But that's why it's important for you to spend some time alone with your Heavenly Father so that He can heal you.

See too many women go from relationship to relationship because of fear of being alone. And this is what the enemy wants because you never get a chance to heal, so that if God sends you the right man you'll run him away. This type of bitterness will cause a lack of trust in men that will not only ruin your relationships, but may hinder your walk with Christ. You may even have trouble receiving the Word from the Man of God just because he's a man. Some women will be skeptical about reading this book, simply because a man wrote it, but you must be careful not to allow the enemy to rob you of your deliverance. You see when you become so afraid of someone hurting you that you refuse to trust even when God says so, what you are really saying is that you have more faith in the enemy's ability to hurt you than God's ability to protect you. Remember trust is not a weakness when your trust is in The Father.

# THE QUESTION

## WHAT'S WRONG WITH ME?
*{I'm Just Not Meant To Be Happy,
I Guess I'll Always Be Alone}*

G od has continued to trouble my spirit about the issues that women face in regards to relationships. Pastor Stephanie and I always seem to find ourselves counseling a woman, who is coming out of, in the middle of, or realizing that she just walked into, a bad relationship or marriage. And the thing that really troubles my spirit is that over the years we've had so many repeat customers. You know the same woman, same story, different man; sure the details may change slightly, but the outcome is always the same. And after a while she begins to wonder is she the problem, saying stuff like, "Why can't I find the right guy, why do I always attract the crazy ones, is there something wrong with me, does God not want me to be happy?" *Some of y'all know what I'm talking about.*

So I began to ask God, "Why is it that so many women go through these cycles? Why is it that they continue to make these poor choices? Why is it that they continue to subject themselves to abuse?" And what God said to me was that, "So many women allow themselves to be used and abused by men simply because they feel like they need a man, like they can't be alone. They've convinced themselves that they can't make it by themselves, and that's why they'll settle for anything." It used to be a man had to be tall, dark, and handsome, and he had to know how to treat a lady just to be considered. Then one day someone made this foolish announcement that there was a shortage of good men, and women began to lower their standards. Then it didn't matter so much what he looked like, he could be two out of the three, he could be tall and dark as long as he treated her right, shoot he could just be dark for that matter if he treated her well she'd still go for it.

Now I know some of you are thinking, "*Now wait a minute Pastor Tucker I couldn't help but notice you said it was a foolish statement that there was a shortage of good men surely with the number of men who are either gay, dead, or in prison you can't disagree with that.*" Well as a Believer surely you can't think that the Creator of all men, the one who created you is incapable of supplying you with a good man. Trust me the problem is not the supply, but where you've been looking, but we'll deal with that issue later. But because you fell for the okey-doke, nowadays it looks like as long as he's a man some of you will take him, because you think being with anybody is better than being alone. But I remember there was an old song that I heard growing up that said "I can do bad by myself". In other words if all he's going to do is be with you and not increase your life, you'd be better off alone.

You see the problem is that the majority of you still have not come to the understanding that if you are a Believer you're not really alone. God said, "He would never leave you nor forsake you", and He's all the Man you'll ever need. Now before you go to the other extreme and think that Pastor Tucker is advocating some perversion, he is not, because there are some who have gone and tried to use their mistreatment by men to justify unnatural relationships with other women, but the Bible tells us that this is not what God intended. Now I know some are of the opinion that this is the way that God created them and this is their right to choose their lifestyle. Well just because it's your right doesn't make it right, and during this age of liberalism and depravity, I think I need to take a moment to deal with this since I'm dealing with restoring our woman. Paul makes it clear in the first chapter of Romans that homosexuality and lesbianism is not the type of relationship God designed for us.

> 25 **Instead of believing what they knew was the truth about God, they deliberately chose to believe lies.** So they worshiped the things God made but not the Creator himself, who is to be praised forever. Amen. 26 **That is why God abandoned them to their shameful desires.** Even the women **turned against the natural way to have sex** and instead indulged in sex with each other. 27 And the men, **instead of** having **normal sexual relationships** with women, burned with lust for each other.

Romans 1:25-27 NLT

Here he tells us that if we choose to deceive ourselves by believing something that we know is not true instead of the word of God that we know is the truth, God will leave us to our own depraved desires. So if you are susceptible to that spirit, the only way you will ever be delivered is to reject the lie that this is a natural relationship, because the word clearly says it is not. So it makes sense why the enemy wants us to believe that people are born that way, and that it's perfectly natural. You may have been born with that depraved desire because you were born in sin, but it's when you chose to believe that it's natural to live that way, instead of believing God's word which you know is true, that He gives you over to that desire. And that's all I'm going to say about that.

Now trust me, Pastor Tucker is not against relationships, but if you are not going to have the kind of relationship that God designed, you'd be better off without one. *Now wait a minute Pastor Tucker are you trying to tell me I'm just supposed to sit around by myself?* Well the truth is too many women never spend enough time alone so they can find out who they are in Christ and what they mean to Him, so they never know what to expect from anybody else, and that's why they accept anything. And that's my assignment to the Body of Christ, to help people reach their divine potential, by teaching them who they are and what they are entitled to as a result of the New Birth.

# THE ANSWER

❦

## YOU DON'T KNOW HOW MUCH YOU'RE WORTH

*{...her price is far above rubies.* **Proverbs 31:10}**

O ne of the main reasons why women make poor choices in men and continue to subject themselves to abusive relationships is because subconsciously, they don't think they deserve any better. They suffer from poor self-image and low self-esteem because they really don't know how much they are worth. They don't understand how valuable they really are. You see most women develop their sense of self-worth from their fathers and how they treated them, but if they didn't have the best example of a father then their perception of their value may be skewed. Sometimes women who have been adopted or discovered that the man who they thought was their father was not, become insecure, they may develop feelings of abandonment and low self-worth. They may struggle with the thought that they did not mean enough to their fathers for him to stick around; that they were of such little value, that he could just give them away. If their fathers left home or never had time for them then they may have grown up feeling unimportant, unworthy of a man's time. If their fathers always criticized and belittled them never listening to what they had to say, then they may have grown up lacking self-confidence thinking that they were incompetent, incapable of thinking for themselves and their voices didn't matter. If they were verbally or physically abused by their fathers, berated about their physical appearance then they may have grown up with a poor body image and low self-esteem, and think that abuse is deserved and should be expected because their actions provoked it. And it's not only how their father treated them, but also how they saw him treat their mother that will affect the treatment that they expect to receive from men.

Because for most women, their relationship with their father was their first relationship with a man, it is the standard by which all others will be measured, and if that relationship was not healthy it can create a void in their life. Like rust on a vehicle, all of these factors may start off as something small, but because they can cause emotional wounds, if left untreated the enemy will take advantage of them to cause major damage. That's why it's important for those of you who did not have the best fatherly example, and even those of you who did, to understand that you have a new Daddy now. You need to know how much you mean to your Heavenly Father. Now what I'm about to share with you will undoubtedly shake your religious upbringing. And if you grew up in the traditional church, for a moment it might disturb you to your core. But the revelation I'm about to share with you will change your relationship with God forever, and eventually every other relationship you enter.

Now I told you it's important for you to understand that you have a new Daddy now, and you need to know how much you mean to your Heavenly Father. Well do you realize that God loves you just as much as He loves Jesus? Now, now, I know to some of you this may sound like blasphemy, but before you go throwing this book across the room, I can prove it to you in scripture. It's right there in John's gospel, it says:

*16 For **God so loved the world that He gave His only begotten Son, that whoever believes** in Him should not perish but have everlasting life.*

John 3:16-17 NKJV

Now if He was willing to give up Jesus in exchange for you, then you had to mean just as much to Him as Jesus did! It's like when you were a kid, and you had a peanut butter and jelly sandwich for lunch, and someone else had a pack of Twinkies. If you were willing to trade your peanut butter and jelly sandwich for a Twinkie, you must have loved Twinkies just as much as you did peanut butter and jelly? Whatever you are willing to give up your most prized possession to get, evidently means just as much to you as your most prized possession.

I know it's hard to believe. That's because the enemy has used low self-esteem, guilt and condemnation to convince you that you are not worthy of God's love; that somehow you deserved the things that were done to you. He's convinced you that the reason why you were raped was because you were dressed the wrong way, or you gave him mixed signals. He's made you believe that you were molested because you spent the night at the wrong friend's house, or because you accepted a quarter from the wrong uncle; that he beat you because you talked back too much, and you know you shouldn't have made him mad. Or maybe you've allowed the enemy to convince you that you were unworthy of love. Simply because your father didn't give you the love you deserved; because you were not born to the right woman, or at the right time in his life, or because you were not a boy, or maybe it's because you reminded him of his mother or his ex-wife. As a result, you felt you had to earn love, so you subjected yourself to unhealthy relationships, looking for love in all the wrong places, but that doesn't mean you have to earn God's love.

Your Heavenly Father loves you regardless of how you perform. The Bible says that He said of Jesus *"This is My beloved Son, in whom I am well pleased."* Matthew 3:17 NKJV And when He said it Jesus had yet to do any miracles, He had yet to heal anyone, He didn't have to do anything to earn His Father's love and neither do you. I already told you He loves you just as much as He loved Jesus. He gave Him up for you, and the Bible says in the eighth chapter of Romans:

*32 He **who did not spare His own Son, but delivered Him up for us all, how shall He not with Him also freely give us all things?***

Romans 8:32 NKJV

So if He gave you His only Son there's nothing He won't do for you because that's how much you mean to Him. It really gives new meaning to the phrase "Daddy's little girl" doesn't it? You see this is why I told you in the last chapter that it is critical for women to learn to spend enough time alone so they can find out who they are in Christ and what they mean to Him, otherwise they will never know what to expect from anybody else. See the problem is because of the void that has been left in their lives by fathers or the lack there of, many women find themselves seeking someone to love and love them. But the real issue is that they neither know how to love or be loved. The truth is their love life is out of order. *What do you mean by that Pastor Tucker?* We've all seen them before, every man she meets she loses her identity; everything is about him, to the point that he becomes her god, all because she loves him *sooo* much. She'll even tell you she loves him more than she loves herself, and she thinks she said something profound and beautiful, but that's because she doesn't know how to love. Jesus makes it clear in Matthew's gospel:

*37 Jesus said to him, "'You shall love the LORD your God with all your heart, with all your soul, and with all your mind.' 38 This is the first and great commandment. 39 And the second is like it: 'You shall love your neighbor as yourself.'*

Matthew 22:37-39 NKJV

Here He gives you the order of your love life. He says love the LORD your God and love your neighbor as yourself. *Well Pastor I thought that meant I was supposed*

*to love others more than myself and put them before me.*
That's not what He said, He said love your neighbor as
yourself. You can't love a man like you love you, until you
first learn how to love you. And you'll never learn how to
love you, until you learn how to love your Father. So many
people never quite understand what that means. See
whenever you spend time learning how to love God you'll
get into the word. Because in order to love God; you have
to love His word. The Bible says, *"In the beginning was
the Word, and the Word was with God, and the Word was
God."* John 1:1 NKJV, so if you are going to love Him you've
got to love His word.

If you love somebody, then you're going to spend some
time with them. So in order to love God with all your heart,
soul, and mind, you must invest your heart, soul, and mind
in His word, but the problem is you've always been too
busy giving your heart, soul, and mind to Joe. You've tried
giving your heart, soul, and mind to Tyrone. You've tried
giving it to Raheem, but that's not what God said, and
that's why you keep running from Joe, to Tyrone, to
Raheem, because you don't understand how to love. You
haven't spent enough time doing what God told you to do.
You didn't spend enough time loving God and His word,
because if you did, you would have learned some stuff
about loving you.

31

See I told you little girls develop their self-worth from their relationships with their fathers and how they treated them. See its natural for little girls to be attached to their daddy; nobody had to teach them they just are born that way, daddy's little girl, seeking his love and affection. Trust me I know what I'm talking about I have two of them. And sure they love their mother, but there's just something about daddy. When they're sleepy they want daddy, when they're hurt they want daddy, when they don't feel good they want daddy, when they're scared they want daddy, because it's just something about daddy that makes them feel secure, there's something about daddy that makes them feel loved. And nobody had to teach them that, since the day they were born they just wanted their daddy, it was just in them. And the thing is, even though they just automatically love daddy, it's how daddy loves them back, that will determine who they are, it's what daddy says about them, that tells them what they are worth, it's how daddy treats them, that teaches them how they deserve to be treated.

And the sad thing is, some of you did not have the best daddy, if you had a daddy at all. But if you would just spend some time loving your real Daddy, if you would just spend some time in His word, then you'd realize what your Daddy has to say about you. You'd know He says you are more precious than rubies. *Wait a minute Pastor are you trying to tell me that I'm more valuable than the stuff I'm trying to get somebody to buy me from the store.* Well that's what your Daddy said. Have you ever noticed when He talks about Christ coming back for His church He calls it His bride. Notice He doesn't say husband. And when He instructs the husband how he should treat his wife, He says husbands love your wives as Christ loved the church. Because we know how much the church means to God, and He wants you to know how much His daughter means to Him as well. And if you spent some time loving your real Daddy, then you'd see how He feels about you, and your sense of self-worth wouldn't be jacked up, because your natural daddy didn't have time for you, because your natural daddy left before you grew up, because your natural daddy beat on your mama and he beat on you, because your natural daddy abused you, because your natural daddy cussed you out, because your natural daddy was an alcoholic, or because your natural daddy was locked up. But once you figure out you got a new Daddy and you spend some time loving your real Daddy then you'll realize how much your Daddy loves you.

Then it says "...*love thy neighbor as thyself.*" Because you can't love no man until you learn how to love you, and you can't learn how to love you, until you learn how to love your Daddy. See because once you learn how to love Daddy, then you'll learn how much you are worth to your Daddy, and you won't let anyone treat you worse than how your Daddy treats you. See if your daddy bought you a BMW when you turned sixteen, then you are not going to let some guy ride you around in a bucket. If your daddy had you living in a house on the hills, then you are not going to let some fool move you into the projects. So if your Daddy said that you're more precious than rubies, you know you're not going to let a man talk to you any kind of way, and he better not even think about putting his hands on you, because you know what you are worth, and you know who you are, you're Daddy's little girl. But the problem is too many of you have not spent enough time with Daddy to see what you are worth. All you know is that your natural daddy never had time for you, so when Tyrone says he's going to hang out with Craig and 'em, that's what you think you deserve. So you don't love you, but you're trying to love him like you love yourself. But if you spend some time loving your Daddy, then you'd learn how to love you, then you could love him like you love yourself. And trust me, you'll be a better woman to him, because you'll know how to love you, but you're going to expect something different from him, and if he can't meet those standards, then he's not the one.

You see whether they admit it or not every woman compares the men she meets to her daddy. And if you're trying to figure out why you keep choosing sorry men, look at the relationship you had with your natural daddy. And if you want to fix it, you need to go back and spend some time with your real Daddy. You've got to develop a relationship with your heavenly Father. The Bible teaches that you were born again not of the flesh or of corruptible seed but of the word, which is incorruptible. So your natural daddy might have been all right, he might have done the best he could, he might have been a rolling stone, but that's all right you got a new Daddy now. And once you recognize how much He loves you, and how much you should love yourself, you'll set a standard for anyone else.

In order to have a healthy relationship you must be able to identify what love is and what love ain't. You see the enemy has taken advantage of low self-esteem, lack of self-love, and popular opinion and made many of you believe that your worth is tied to a man, that your identity is defined in a man, so that you think you are incomplete without one, and that's why you spend so much of your time and energy looking for one to love, but you can no longer accept abuse and mistreatment masquerading in the name of love, because you mean too much to your Father and nothing but the best will do for Daddy's little girl.

# THE BEGINNING

## HOW DID I GET LIKE THIS?
*{You Know You Gotta Have A Man,*
*You Can't Make It By Yourself}*

I see so many women who seem to go through periods of depression when they don't have a man, but then when they have one their happiness is short lived, because it's only a matter of time before he's cheating on her, mistreating her, abusing her, and she's miserable all over again. Sound familiar? By now some of you are probably beginning to wonder is there a curse on your family. Because as far you can remember all the women in your family have had trouble in their relationships. Your mother dated sorry men, your grandmother dated sorry men, your aunts, your cousins, and now it looks like you have been doomed to repeat the process but how did this foolishness get started.

Well they start off making poor choices, and when that relationship fails, of course they set out in search of another, because God forbid they actually be alone, and then they make another mistake, and the cycle continues. Until finally they get to an age where they are afraid that they will end up alone so they settle for whoever they can get no matter how he treats them because we all know *"a woman needs a man."* And the young girls grow up watching this pattern and repeat it.

Well guess what, that was never your Father's will for your life. You see the enemy has been deceiving women for a long time. And it might not have started with you, but it can STOP with you. If you receive this revelation, you can make sure that your daughters, your nieces, your cousins, and let's be real, even your own mothers will not have to go through this again. So let's go back to the beginning:

*3:1 Now **the serpent was more cunning** than any beast of the field which the LORD God had made. And **he said to the woman,** "Has God indeed said, 'You shall not eat of every tree of the garden'?" 2 And the woman said to the serpent, "We may eat the fruit of the trees of the garden; 3 but of the fruit of the tree which is in the midst of the garden, God has said, 'You shall not eat of it, nor shall you touch it, lest you die.'" 4 Then the serpent said to the woman, "**You will not surely die. 5 For God knows that in*** *the day you eat of it your eyes will be opened, and <u>you will</u>* *<u>be like God</u>, <u>knowing good and evil</u>." 6 So when the* *woman saw that the tree was good for food, that it was* *pleasant to the eyes, and a tree desirable to make one wise,* *she took of its fruit and ate. She also gave to her husband* *with her, and he ate. 7 Then the eyes of both of them were* *opened, and they knew that they were naked; and they* *sewed fig leaves together and made themselves coverings.*

Genesis 3:1-7 NKJV

Now here we have the woman's first encounter with the enemy. And he says to her in verse 5 *"For God knows that in the day you eat of it your eyes will be opened, and <u>you</u>* *<u>will be like God</u>",* Now does the Bible not tell us in **Genesis 1:26** that when God created them, **"*he created them male and female in the image of God He created them.*"** So when he tells her **"*<u>you will be like God</u>"*,** she was already like God, but he tricked her into believing that she was less than who God said she was, and that she needed something that she already had. He said *"**knowing** **good and evil**",* now being that she had been created in the image of God, she already knew good, and the Bible teaches us that God knows no evil, so she was already like God, so everything she needed to be like God she already had, but he tricked her into believing that she was less than

39

who God said she was, and that she needed something she did not need. So she accepted a perversion or imitation. She accepted a perversion of good, which was evil. So when she saw that the tree was good for food, and it was pleasant to the eye and the tree was desirable to make one wise, she took the fruit and she ate it. She fell for it.

You've got to make up your mind right now, that you will never allow him to convince you again that you are less than who your Father says you are, or that you need something that your Father has already given you, because if you do, his days of taking advantage of you are over.

Now I told you earlier that God said the reason why so many women allow themselves to be used and abused by men is because they feel like they need a man, like they can't be alone, like they can't make it by themselves and that the enemy has taken advantage of low self-esteem, lack of self-love, and popular opinion and made many of you believe that your worth is tied to a man, that your identity is defined in a man, so that you think you are incomplete without one. Well can I prove it to you?

I get so tired of women saying that they got to have a man, that they need a man in their life, that they need a man to complete them. So when God spoke this revelation in my spirit I have not been able to sleep since. God makes it clear in Genesis chapter two:

# THE BEGINNING

*18 And the LORD God said, **It is not good that <u>the man</u> should be alone**; I will make him an help meet for him.*

Genesis 2:18 KJV

So who needed who? It says here that the man needed someone, so God created you for him, not vice versa. So at what point did it say that a woman shouldn't be by herself. God declared that it was not good for the man to be alone. But the enemy has convinced you that you can't be by yourself, that if you spend too much time alone you're an old maid, that there's something wrong with you. Your girlfriends will even tell you, "Girl, you need a man! You can't make it by yourself! It ain't good for you to be by yourself!" Your mama even told you, "Child it ain't good for no woman to be by herself! You need a man in your life! You need somebody to keep your bed warm!" Well who told you that lie? The Bible says, "*It is not good that <u>the man</u> should be alone*"; He said "*I will make a help meet for <u>him</u>.*" He needed somebody; God created you for him not vice versa. So you had better stop listening to that foolishness and get yourself together! But the enemy has you believing that you need a man to complete you, that you're not whole without one. Well let's see what God has to say:

# DAMAGED GOODS

*21 And the LORD God caused a deep sleep to fall upon Adam and he slept: and **he took one of his ribs**, and closed up the flesh instead thereof; 22 And the rib, which the LORD God had taken from man, made he a woman, and brought her unto the man.23 And Adam said, This is now bone of my bones, and flesh of my flesh: she shall be called Woman, because she was taken out of Man.*

Genesis 2:21-23 KJV

Now here we see where the woman is being made and the Bible says, God put the man to sleep, took a rib out of him, then it says that He took the rib that He had taken from the man and made the woman. Now think about this for a moment. If I have a gallon of milk, and I get a measuring cup, and I pour out a pint of milk, do I have a whole pint? *Yes.* Do I have a whole gallon? *No.* Which one is incomplete? The gallon. So if I took a rib out of the whole man and made a whole woman, what do I have left? *A man with a missing rib!* But the enemy has told you, you are incomplete without a man. So you keep running around talking about, "I gotta find me a man! My life is incomplete because I don't have a man!" Well, who is missing a rib? I'm trying to help somebody!

You've allowed the enemy to deceive you and because of this, you are allowing yourself to be used and abused!

You have got to recognize who you arc in Christ Jcsus, God created you with a purpose; He made you to complete man, to accompany man, to be his help meet, to help him fulfill his purpose in life. He made you because man needs you, not because you needed someone to run around behind, not because your life was incomplete, so you need to understand your purpose. Because if you don't understand your purpose, you will continue to subject yourself to a cycle of unhealthy relationships, chasing after something that you think that you need, because if you don't know the purpose of something abuse is inevitable. And that's not what your Daddy desires for your life.

# THE QUEST

ご

## WHY CAN'T I FIND A GOOD MAN?
*{Looking For Love In All The Wrong Places!}*

N ow for as long as I can recall I have heard women complaining about the lack of good men. You may be one of the women who have asked themselves the question "Why can't I find a good man?" Because the enemy has convinced you that there is a shortage of good men, that all of the good men are married and the rest are either gay, dead, or in prison. *Well Pastor that's true, and if that's not the case then they just ain't no good.* Well I told you earlier if you are a believer surely you can't think that the creator of all men, the one who created you is incapable of supplying you with a good man, and that the problem is not the supply, but where you've been looking. *Well Pastor, don't keep me in suspense.* Well in order to answer the sixty-four million dollar question we'll have to look at the eighteenth chapter of Proverbs.

# DAMAGED GOODS

*22 **He who finds a wife finds a good thing**, And **obtains favor** from the LORD.*

Proverbs 18:22 NKJV

Now I told you in the last chapter when God created woman, He put the man to sleep and took out a rib and made the woman from the rib. So now you have a man that is missing a rib, and a woman who is made from that rib. So according to the scriptures, the man is the one that is incomplete. Now if something is missing, what do you do? *You go looking for it.* Now the Bible says, in verse 22 *"He who finds a wife finds a good thing,"* so if my rib is missing, who ought to be looking; *I should.* So to answer your question "Why can't you find a good man?" You shouldn't be looking in the first place. The Bible says "... *He who finds a wife"* the reason why you are always finding the wrong man is because the enemy sees you looking for something God didn't tell you to look for. And when you try to find something that God hasn't told you to look for, the enemy is always willing to help you find it.

You see you have some people that try to get all spiritual and say, "I wish the Lord would just lead me by a voice, but that's not what God said, the Bible says *"The spirit of a man is the lamp of The Lord..."* Proverbs 20:27 NKJV So God is going to lead you by the spirit, but if you

46

want to be lead by voices, the enemy says I got this, I'll handle it, they want a voice, I will give 'em a voice, and the next thing they know they find themselves following around demonic spirits, sitting in somebody's psychiatric unit. That's why you've got to be careful about looking for something that God didn't tell you to look for. You see God said, *"He who finds a wife finds a good thing..."* You need to understand the quality of what you are. He didn't say he would find just anything, but a good thing! So you need to stop allowing him to treat you like anything, and stop allowing him to call you anything. You see it really bothers me to hear how our young men refer to our women as females, but what bothers me even more is that you all accept it. You need to understand a female is not who you are or what you are, that's your sex, but you answer to it, so no wonder they try and treat you like it's your purpose. Talking about "You the finest female I ever met." acting like he said something nice to you. You need to ask him, "Who do you think you are talking to?" But when you allow him to refer to you as a bi_ ch, which is a female dog, no wonder the men you attract are of the K9 variety.

You need to stop agreeing with the enemy, God called you a woman which is the opposite and completion of man, his counter part, his missing piece, the one he needs, so he needs to learn to treat you like it. You've got to recognize what the word says about you, it says he *"...obtains favor from the Lord."* that means that God did something good for him, that God blessed him when he found you. I told you earlier when I married Pastor Stephanie I knew what I got. I knew God had blessed me, that He had given me a gift. You see I understood that God was entrusting me with His daughter, I was not thinking about her parents, I was thinking that's God's daughter. I told you, people laugh when they see me crying on the video, but that's because I recognized what God was doing for me. I realized I must have obtained favor with Him, in order for Him to give me His daughter, because I recognized what she meant to Him. You need to recognize your value. The Bible says,*"...a wise, understanding, and prudent wife is from the Lord"* Proverbs 19:14 AMP, that means you're a gift, and not just any old gift, but a gift from God, so you need to act like it. Don't just give yourself to anybody, to any undeserving joker. And since you are a gift from God, you need to let God decide who you belong to. Now we know that the Bible says that *"Every good and perfect gift is from above, coming down from the Father..."* James 1:17 NIV, so in order to be considered a gift from God, that means that God had to say that you were something special. And we know He just said that *"...a wise, understanding, and prudent wife is from the Lord"* Proverbs 19:14 AMP, so if God's going to bestow a gift of that caliber, He's only going to bestow it on somebody He thinks is deserving. See you are always worrying about the type of man you are getting, and that's the problem. Because you are worried about who you are going to give yourself to, but if God is going to reward somebody, He is only going to reward somebody who is deserving. So all you've got to do is stay in His word and be the gift that He told you to be. All you have to do is be wise, understanding, and prudent. And since you know that He is not just going to give His precious gifts to anybody, whoever He gives you to is going to deserve you.

See that's the problem, you are doing all of the looking, when God never told you to look for anything, because He said *"He who finds a wife obtains favor from the Lord."* See God is not going to let him find you, unless he deserves you. But if you show him where you are, if you keep exposing yourself, there's no telling who might get you. If you've ever watched one of those shows on television where the police are trying to protect the witness from the bad guys and place them into protective custody. Then all of a sudden the bad guys show up, so the police go after them and tell the witness to stay in the car, but sure enough the witness gets out and the bad guys kidnap the witness. Well it's not the police's fault, if they had only stayed hidden, if they would have only stayed in the car, they would have made it into protective custody, but instead they ended up in the hands of the enemy.

God said if you allow me to handle it, just follow my instructions the one who finds you, will have obtained favor from me. God said all these years I've been trying to keep you hidden, but you kept exposing yourself. As a matter of fact Pastor Stephanie and I had been in the same room three times before and never met, because God said that I was not ready for her, He kept her hidden from me, until I was deserving of the reward, but she could have exposed herself, all you have to do is stay in the will of God, be the gift that He told you to be, keep trusting God, and God said the man who finds you will deserve you. The Bible says, *"Who can find a virtuous woman?"* Proverbs 31:10 KJV, meaning a virtuous woman is hard to come by. So if he's going to get you, he's going to need God's help. If you just remain virtuous then only someone who God has assisted will find you.

You see because you are valuable to God, as a matter of fact in Proverbs chapter 12 He tells us, ***"An excellent wife is the crown of her husband…"*** Proverbs 12:4 NKJV You see a crown is the display of the king's splendor, and although every king may wear a crown, God only places a crown on those He anoints; those that He says are supposed to be king. You remember David and Saul both were kings, both wore crowns, the people chose Saul and God told them that he would mistreat them, but God chose David as a man after his own heart, a man deserving of the crown, and the people were blessed by him. You see you've got to understand who you are, and what you represent, so you won't make choices where you end up mistreated, but instead know that God knows what's best for you, because you are worth too much. Paul makes this clear in the Corinthian letter.

*7 For a man indeed ought not to cover his head, since he is the image and glory of God; but **woman is the glory of man**. 8 For man is not from woman, but woman from man. 9 Nor was **man created for the woman, but woman for the man**.*

1 Corinthians 11:7-9 NKJV

Here he tells us that man is the representation of God, he is God's greatest achievement, he's God's treasure, but it says that woman is the glory of man, she is the representation of the man, she is his greatest achievement, she's his treasure, that's why we say that she is our better half, when people see Pastor Stephanie, they know that I must be some kind of man to have a wife like that. And I am blessed to have her; you need to recognize that the man that God favors with you is blessed to have you.

The Bible says " *9 Neither was man created on account of or for the benefit of woman, but **woman** on account of and **for the benefit of man**.* " 1 Corinthians 11:9 AMP You were created for his benefit, not him for yours, man is not your glory, you don't need a man to make you look good, you are the treasure, the achievement, the thing that makes him look good. You are the thing that makes people look and see what kind of man he is. So there is no way you can be defined in him, man is not your glory. As a matter of fact Paul says in verse *"15 But if a woman has long hair, it is a glory to her;"* 1 Corinthians 11:15 NKJV So a man is not your glory, your hair is, so you better forget about looking for a man and go get your hair done! Because the Lord said you can look good all by yourself. But you have been so busy trying to find someone to love that you missed the one who loves you. Now in order to illustrate this next point I'm going to show you something in a familiar scripture. Now you might think I'm crazy, but I need you to use your spiritual imagination, and trust me, God's going to reveal something to you. Now in John's gospel we find Jesus' encounter with the woman at the well and in verse five it says:

**John 4:5-30**

*5 So He came to a city of Samaria which is called Sychar, near the plot of ground that Jacob gave to his son Joseph. 6 Now Jacob's well was there. Jesus therefore, being wearied from His journey, sat thus by the well. It was about the sixth hour. 7 A woman of Samaria came to draw water. **Jesus said to her, "Give Me a drink."***

Now most women who are looking for a man have already decided who they are looking for. He's got to look like this and he's got to drive that and he 's got to have this kind of hair. Now I know some of you are thinking, *Pastor I'm not that shallow.* Well you may not be, but trust me most women have some characteristics, some criteria, that they are basing their selection on. They have created a mental picture frame, and they are trying to find someone who fits in it. Now don't get me wrong there's nothing wrong with having standards, I told you earlier you must establish some, but the problem is, because the criteria you are using has been derived from the world, the one you are looking for is all wrong. Now let's forget for a moment that this is Jesus, imagine that this is an ordinary woman meeting an ordinary man in an "establishment" that happens to serve beverages. Now the majority of women would be looking for either one of two things to transpire, either for him to ask you can he buy you a drink, or for you to ask him to buy you a drink, the last thing you would be looking for is for him to ask **you** to buy **him** a drink. Let's just be real, because that would automatically disqualify him; that would immediately let you know he's not the one.

**It says** *8 For His disciples had gone away into the city to buy food. 9 Then the woman of Samaria said to Him, "How is it that You, being a Jew, ask a drink from me, a Samaritan woman?" For Jews have no dealings with Samaritans.*

Immediately she tells him he's not her type. He don't even look like she thinks he is supposed to look, he doesn't have the right kind of hair, he doesn't have the right complexion, he isn't her type of guy, he is not the guy she is looking for.

**It says** *10 Jesus answered and said to her, "If you knew the gift of God, and who it is who says to you, 'Give Me a drink,' you would have asked Him, and He would have given you living water."*

Now if we didn't know this was Jesus we would've thought, he was putting down some serious game. Like,

*"Girl, don't you realize I am the gift of God. I'm God's gift and if you knew who it was I would've bought you the best drink you ever had."*...Now she becomes intrigued... and once again begins "sizing him up"

**It says** *11 The woman said to Him, "Sir, You have nothing to draw with, and the well is deep. Where then do You get that living water?*

In other words, *"He ain't got no money, I didn't see him pull up in anything, and if he had some money, why did he ask me to buy him a drink in the first place. He broke! He ain't got nothing!"* Because of course that's her mentality, she's thinking like everyone else in the world...stay with me now.

**It says** *12 Are You greater than our father Jacob, who gave us the well, and drank from it himself, as well as his sons and his livestock?"*

She automatically compares him to her father, now remember I told you, most women whether they want to admit it or not, compare the men they meet to their daddy. She says *"are you better than my daddy? At least he could buy by the bottle."*

**It says** *13 Jesus answered and said to her, "Whoever drinks of this water will thirst again, 14 but whoever drinks of the water that I shall give him will never thirst. But the water that I shall give him will become in him a fountain of water springing up into everlasting life." 15 The woman said to Him, "Sir, give me this water, that I may not thirst, nor come here to draw."*

He says to her *"Look here girl, you just don't understand the kind of drinks I got. I could buy you a bottle of this stuff and you'd still be thirsty but if you just had a glass of what I got you'd be straight."* So she's like, *"alright I hear you. Go ahead and pour me some, and let me see what you are working with"*, but then He checks her.

**It says** *16 Jesus said to her, "**Go, call your husband, and come here**."*

Now once again because she's in the world, she is like *"Oh he's trying to play me, he just wants to see if I am married."* But check her answer.

**It says** *17 The woman answered and said, **"I have no husband."***

Now notice she said nothing about the man that she was living with, she had already decided he was gone, *"If this man is for real, then Raheem is getting kicked out when I get home"*.

*Jesus said to her, "You have well said, 'I have no husband,' 18 **for you have had five husbands, and the one whom you now have is not your husband;** in that you spoke truly."*

Now she is like, "Aw wait a minute now, this guy knows some stuff that he has no business knowing."

*19 The woman said to Him, "Sir, I perceive that You are a prophet.*

She is like *"oh Lord this must be the preacher"*, so now she has gone spiritual.

*20 Our fathers worshiped on this mountain, and you Jews say that in Jerusalem is the place where one ought to worship."*

Now let's look at this for a moment, she has had five husbands and she is living with a dude now, so she has been looking for something. There is some kind of void in her life, if not she would not have had five husbands and another man at home. And there's still a void in her life and she's looking for somebody to fill it. Now at first she did not think that Jesus would qualify, but once he had shown her *"he had game"*, she was willing to play along with the game until she found out. But once she found out that he was the preacher, she began to address the true void in her life, she starts talking about worship, she starts to expose the fact that her relationship is lacking.

You see that's how most women are, busy going from man to man trying to fill a void, and won't give Jesus the time of day, because he didn't approach you like everyone else, instead of offering you something that wouldn't last he required something of you; so that in return he could give you what you really needed, but until you get real and address the real void in your life, you'll continue to be so busy looking for somebody to love, that you miss the one who loves you. Yeah, I know it looked like I was just telling a funny story, but it's always all fun and games until God gets serious.

**It says** *21 Jesus said to her, "Woman, believe Me, the hour is coming when you will neither on this mountain, nor in Jerusalem, worship the Father. 22 You worship what* *you do not know; we know what we worship, for salvation is of the Jews. 23 But the hour is coming, and now is, when the true worshipers will worship the Father in spirit and truth; **for the Father is seeking such** to worship Him.*

He told her while you are busy looking for something, God is actually looking for you.

He said *24 God is Spirit, and those who worship Him must worship in spirit and truth." 25 The woman said to Him, **"I know that Messiah is coming"** (who is called Christ). **"When He comes, He will tell us all things."***

So she tells him, I know that the perfect man is coming, and when he comes he is going to tell me all the stuff that I want to hear, but she still missed it, he was staring her right in the face, see she was so busy looking for what she wanted, that she missed Jesus. I told you when I started this that she was so busy looking for someone to love that she missed the one who loves her.

**It says** *26 Jesus said to her, "I who speak to you am He."*

**Then it says** *28 The woman then left her waterpot, went her way into the city, and said to the **men**, 29 "Come,* *see a Man who told me all things that I ever did. Could this be the Christ?" 30 Then they went out of the city and came to Him.*

Now in verse 28 it says that she *"said to the men"*, well here the Greek for men is anthropos, which means people. So she went to talk to the people, not the just the men. And I believe that when she went back to town, she went and told some of the girls she used to roll with, the girls she used to hit the clubs and pick up men with, and she told them come see a man. Because if you've had some issues, and you've been delivered from your issues, you ought to want to help the folks you know that are still stuck where you came from.

You see when I met Pastor Stephanie; I tried to convince all my boys that settling down was the thing to do. When I got saved I wanted all my boys to be saved. So I imagine this woman went back to the girls she used to roll with. And I'm sure that some of them got excited, because they probably thought, "Child, Stella got her a new man. She must have put Raheem out." And when she told them he told me everything I ever did, they said, "Girl, he's a good man, an understanding man, I got to find me one of them. He don't judge her for nobody she been with, or nothing she done he must be sensitive." You know cause

Jesus is like that, He won't judge you for what you've done, He won't judge you for where you've been, He's just gone love you for who you are. Just ask the woman caught in the act of adultery. He just sat there writing in the sand, while everybody else talked about her, then He asked her is there no one left to condemn you, then neither do I, cause that's the kind of man He is. Then she said, "...*could this be the Christ*", and they said, "Chiiiild, she done went and got herself a preacher." But trust me, it won't that type of party. The Bible says, "Then they went out of the city and came to Him." Now some of them might have come just to see if it was true, others came just to see if he had any brothers, but when they got there it says in verse 39:

*39And many of the Samaritans of that city believed in Him because of the word of the woman who testified, "He told me all that I ever did." 40 So when the Samaritans had come to Him, they urged Him to stay with them; and He stayed there two days. 41 And many more believed because of His own word. 42 Then they said to the woman, "Now we believe, not because of what you said, for we ourselves have heard Him and we know that this is indeed the Christ, the Savior of the world."*

NKJV

Now I imagine that these were women that were just like her, they had tried and failed, looked for love in all the wrong places, would be with anybody so they would not have to be by themselves, but they found out that Jesus was all the man they ever needed. They fell in love with Him for themselves. They found out they didn't need no man to complete them. And guess what you don't either can I prove it to you. Paul tells us in the Colossian letter.

*8 Beware lest anyone cheat you through philosophy and empty deceit, according to the tradition of men, according to the basic principles of the world, and not according to Christ. 9 For in Him dwells all the fullness of the Godhead bodily; 10 and **you are complete in Him**, who is the head of all principality and power.*

Colossians 2:8-10 NKJV

Did you see that? You are complete in Him. Ladies don't you ever let the enemy tell you, you can't make it by yourself, that you can't be alone, that you need a man, Jesus is all the man you'll ever need. Why don't you let me introduce you to Him?

If you have never accepted Jesus Christ, as your personal Lord and Savior, pray this prayer:

Lord Jesus,

I ask You to come into my life and forgive me of all my sins. I confess my sins before You this day. I denounce satan and all his works. I confess Jesus as the Lord of my life. Thank You for saving me. Fill me with Your Holy Spirit. I believe with my heart and I confess with my mouth that You rose from the dead. Now I am saved."

You have now been adopted into God's family. You are no longer bound to sin or to the old nature, you're a new creation in Christ Jesus. The next step is to get connected to a good Bible-believing Bible-teaching church. So you can learn, grow and work together to help build the kingdom of God. And remember you have a new Daddy now and He loves you because you are Daddy's little Girl.

# THE RESTORATION

✍

## THERE'S NOTHING LIKE THE FATHER'S LOVE!
### *{Daddy Kiss It, Make It Better}*

Well now that you know who you are and how much you mean to your Father, you'll never accept abuse or mistreatment again, you won't make the poor choices that put you in those unhealthy relationships, but if you're not careful you still won't be happy. *What do you mean Pastor?* You see your journey is not over, you still have to recover from the damage that has already been done. For years the enemy has been trying to destroy you, and isolation and shame have been two of his most successful strategies. He made you believe that no one understood what you were going through, and that's why every time you were in the midst of an unhealthy relationship you would withdraw from your friends and family, especially those who cared about you, who were supportive of you, those who were in the Lord and would offer sound advice. Because he would convince you that they didn't understand and that you shouldn't bother them with your problems. When the truth is his goal was to isolate you from your help so he could destroy you. That's why the Bible tells us to *"Be sober, be vigilant; because your adversary the devil walks about like a roaring lion, seeking whom he may devour."* 1 Peter 5:8 NKJV And if you have ever watched a documentary about lions and how they hunt then you'd know that their strategy is to isolate their prey from the herd. They will pick out one of the small, the weak, the slow, or the wounded from the herd and once they separate him from the rest, he's dinner.

Now I know what you are thinking. *Pastor I have plenty of friends.* Yeah, but the friends you talk to are just like you. They are in the same situations: abused, mistreated, lonely, bad relationship to bad relationship, because misery loves company. But you see the Bible says *"Blessed is the man Who walks not in the counsel of the ungodly, Nor stands in the path of sinners, Nor sits in the seat of the scornful;"* Psalms 1:1 NKJV So the first thing you need to do is change who you are listening to. You've got to get away from people who are negative because they will affect your thinking. See you think that y'all are supporting each other, but what you are really doing is having a pity party continuing to reinforce each other's negative mentality. That's why you've got to seek Godly counsel, and let me let you in on a little secret, if the advice begins with the phrase *"Girl, if I were you…"* then it's not Godly, because Godly counsel will always confirm what God has already told you in His word. So if they are speaking doubt and disbelief, then you are talking to the wrong people. See you must be careful who you associate with, because you've been delivered. And if you continue to listen to the same people you have been, although God has healed you, you'll find yourself relapsing. Because the Bible is clear *"Do not be misled: "Bad company corrupts good character.""* 1 Corinthians 15:33-34 NIV

The other strategy that the enemy has used against you is shame. He has made you feel guilty about the things that have been done to you, about the decisions you've made, even ashamed of your current condition. But the Bible says, *"There is therefore now no condemnation to those who are in Christ Jesus…"* Romans 8:1 NKJV I told you earlier that when the woman was caught in the act of adultery He didn't condemn her so He doesn't condemn you either. As a matter of fact Jesus himself told us in John's gospel that He didn't come to condemn the world but to save it. You see it is the enemy that is the accuser of the brethren, so if you are feeling guilty you can be certain those feeling didn't come from the Father. See if you are going to walk in the fullness of your restoration forgiveness is the key to getting your life back. And the first person you must forgive is you. Sure you've made some poor choices, who hasn't, but the wonderful thing about God is that no matter what you did, you can always start over. He says in 1 John chapter one:

*9 If we confess our sins, He is faithful and just to forgive us our sins and to cleanse us from all unrighteousness.*

1 John 1:9 NKJV

And not only that He tells us through the prophet Isaiah:

25 "I, even I, am He who blots out your transgressions for My own sake; And **I will not remember your sins.**

Isaiah 43:25 NKJV

But the problem is you won't forget what you did wrong, and you keep letting the enemy remind you of it and blaming God for it. As if God is holding it over your head, I told you he has tricked you, but you've got to let it go. You've got to accept the fact that you've been forgiven and make up your mind that you will not be tormented by your past errors or mistakes. Stop allowing the enemy to remind you of your past, it's called your past for a reason. Because if you are not careful, you will let your past infect your present and destroy your future.

In order to become completely whole, you must forgive the ones who hurt you no matter what they did. *But Pastor you don't understand, you don't know what they did to me.* Well you're right, I don't know, but as long as you refuse to forgive the people who hurt you, you give them the power to keep you in bondage. You see the people who hurt you; they have gone on about their business by now. They may be happily married with children, but you are miserable. They go to sleep every night, while you're having nightmares and pacing the floor. While they are developing meaningful relationships, you're the one who has trust issues. Even if they are hurting someone else, you are old news to them, they have moved on, but you are still stuck. And you'll never be able to go forward until you forgive them. I know some of you are thinking, *"I've moved past it, I've gone on with my life."* Well if that were true you wouldn't have read this far. But before you get mad and miss your deliverance, let me help you.

See whenever you get hurt you are faced with two options. The first option says I can take away the pain right away and you don't have to do anything, and nobody will ever be able to hurt you again. The second option says I too can take away the pain, but its going to take some time and effort on your part, and there is no guarantee you'll never get hurt again, but if you do, this offer will always be available. Now most people choose option one, because who would not want to get rid of the pain without having to do anything, and have a guarantee never to be hurt again, but the problem is you didn't know there was a catch. See the enemy told you he could make the pain go away by making you bitter, and hardening your heart so you become numb, and no one could ever hurt you again, you never have to feel that kind of pain again, but what he didn't tell you is that now that your heart is hardened, now that you are numb, you'll never feel love again either. See it's like having the doctor tell you he can get rid of the pain in your leg immediately, but the catch is he didn't tell you he was going to amputate your leg. So not only do you get rid of the pain, but you also lose the ability to walk. But with the second option even though it's more difficult, God says if you will forgive, it may be painful to have to relive what they did to you, but when it's all said and done, you'll get your life back. And just because you forgive them doesn't mean what they did to you was right; it doesn't mean you deserved it. It means that even though they did something horrible to you, you are not going to allow them to hold you hostage with it as well, so in obedience to your Father, you forgive them, which allows him to now minister to you. See Jesus tells us in Mark's gospel:

*"... whenever you stand praying, if you have anything against anyone, forgive him, that your Father in heaven may also forgive you your trespasses. 26 But if you do not forgive, neither will your Father in heaven forgive your trespasses."*

Mark 11:25-26 NKJV

So if you won't forgive them, God won't forgive you and you'll never be free from condemnation and guilt. You see God can't answer your prayers to take away the pain as long as you refuse to forgive the one who caused it. By holding on to unforgiveness you are holding on to pain. And God says in time you'll forget all about what they did. *Well Pastor I don't know about that, I may forgive but I can't forget.* Well the Bible says in the ninth chapter of Hebrews:

*14 how much more shall the blood of Christ, who through the eternal Spirit offered Himself without spot to God, cleanse your conscience from dead works...*

Hebrews 9:14 NKJV

You see the blood of Christ has the ability to brain wash you. If you just spend enough time with your Father His love can help you not only forgive but forget. And even though there is no guarantee you'll never be hurt again, His offer is still available. You see rehab is always a better option than amputation, and if you allow God to send you the man that He has selected for His daughter, you are less likely to be hurt. No matter how badly you've been wounded, mistreated or abused, the Father's love has the ability to restore you. It's like when you were a little child no matter the size of the bruise, cut, or scrape there was something magic about daddy's kisses, all he had to do was kiss it to make it better. And it's the same with your Heavenly Father that's why you must remember Father knows best and how much He loves you, because no matter what you'll always be Daddy's Little Girl. And no matter how badly you've been damaged, there's nothing like the restoring power of the Father's love to make you whole again.

Below or somewhere more private I suggest that you list the names of the people who have hurt you, and what they did to you and go to your Father in prayer, give Him the opportunity to heal you. Begin first by forgiving yourself, and then forgive them for what they did to you. Remember you are not saying that what they did was right, or that it was OK, but that you refuse to allow them to hold you hostage any longer and in obedience to your Father you will forgive them and allow Him to handle it. Next continue to plead the blood of Jesus over what they did to you and every time the enemy tries to bring it back to your remembrance just continue to plead the blood of Jesus over it.

### *List of Repairs*

_____

_____

_____

_____

_____

_____

_____

_____

_____

_____

_____

_____

_____

_____

_____

_____

Now trust me I'm not crazy enough to believe that just because you wrote their names down and what they did to you that you have forgiven them, that's just the beginning of the process. I told you it was going to take effort on your part. The Bible teaches us that to be delivered from some demons it's going to require prayer and fasting. You're going to have to continue to pray, fast, and commit yourself to the word if you are going to see a full restoration.

Can I be honest with you for a moment? Some of you are reading this book because someone shared it with you, because you were tired of your situation, and you are reading with the hope that your life will be changed, but the truth is your life won't change until you change your life. *What do you mean Pastor?* Well for many of you up until now, the church has been just a building that you go to sometimes, if you have time, and the Bible is just the book that the preacher preaches from. But if you expect your life to change you've got to recognize that God designed this system for your life to be successful and the reason why you've been struggling is because you haven't been using the system. You're going to have to commit yourself to reading and studying God's word because as I told you before in order to love the Father, you've got to love His word. You've got to seek Him for where He would have you to be connected, because contrary to popular belief it does matter where you go to church.

I know for some of you this may come as a shock, but what's good for mama ain't necessarily good for you. You need to be in a Bible-believing Bible-teaching church; that is if you expect to see change. Because church was meant to change your life and if it's not, you need to change your church. And by committing yourself to the things of God, God will remove the pain just as He promised. He's the only one who can truly teach you how to forgive. Because people say that they have forgiven, that they have moved on, but they really haven't, they are just walking in buried resentment, and it's only a matter of time before it surfaces.

Now the true test of whether or not you have truly forgiven the one who hurt you is, when you see them does the pain and animosity return? If someone mentions their name do you still get upset? If not then your heart is clear. Because when you have forgiven someone, he could pass you on the street with another woman and it wouldn't bother you at all. Now that's not to say you'll never struggle with painful thoughts again. But the Bible says we have the power to *"...take captive every thought to make it obedient to Christ."* 2 Corinthians 10:5 NIV That's why it's important to be properly connected and remain consistent in your walk with Christ, because not only will it help you forgive, but it will teach you how to trust again. Because God doesn't just want to heal you He wants to restore you.

See many of you have been hurt by the things you've seen and experienced to the point that you lost all trust in men. You've become guarded in your dealings, and you'll never be able to have a real relationship if you don't learn how to trust. You see the reason that many women end up in the situations that they are in is because of what they witnessed growing up. They saw their mothers mistreated by their fathers or other men, and they were taught not to trust men, but at the same time because they watched them accept abuse and mistreatment they learned to expect it as well, and the example that was set before them, framed their thinking. That's why even though you have forgiven you still have trouble trusting, because that's what you were taught, but I told you God wants to restore you. Paul tells us in the Roman letter:

*2 **Do not conform any longer to the pattern of this world**, but **be transformed by the renewing of your mind**. Then you will be able to test and approve what God's will is-his good, pleasing and perfect will.*

Romans 12:2 NIV

76

In other words, you can't follow the old pattern any longer. I don't care what mama told you, I don't care what auntie said. That's not what God said, and that's why it's important to be in the house of God, with the man and woman of God that God has chosen for your life. You see God ordained that relationship for your life to help restore you. He gave you a spiritual mother and father so that they could teach you what the word of God said, and show you a biblical example of what marriage is supposed to be, so you could see how a man is supposed to treat a woman. Now I know somebody may be thinking, *"Well Pastor I don't mean no harm, but my pastor's marriage is just as tore up as my relationships."* Well I know I may lose some readers right here, but the truth shall set you free. That's why I told you, you had better seek God about where He desired you to be connected because the word teaches us that the anointing flows from the head down, and Paul said, when writing the qualifications of a pastor, that he must be:

*"...the husband of but one wife, temperate, self-controlled, respectable, hospitable, able to teach, 3 not given to drunkenness, not violent but gentle, not quarrelsome, not a lover of money. 4 He must manage his own family well and see that his children obey him with*

*proper respect. 5(If anyone does not know how to manage his own family, how can he take care of God's church?)"*

1 Tim 3:2-5 NIV

So in other words the pastor has got to be a good example of a husband. If the pastor is not a good husband, he's not a good pastor. And that's all I got to say about that. God made it clear through the prophet Jeremiah:

*"And I will give you pastors according to mine heart, which shall feed you with knowledge and understanding."*

Jeremiah 3:15 KJV

You see the purpose of your spiritual parents is to teach you the word of God so that your mind can be renewed. And then and only then will you know God's will for your life. You'll know who you are in Christ and how much you mean to your Father. And when you are connected where God has placed you, you'll have pastors with a heart after God's, so that you can experience what it is like to have a man concerned about you, and not trying to hurt or take advantage of you. You'll have a spiritual mother to teach you how to be a woman of worth, and how to you walk in purity and wisdom as you are waiting for your Boaz that God is preparing for you. And through the love of Christ you'll learn to trust again, but you've got to be where He put you. You see the purpose of the church, the word, and the man and woman of God are to help teach you how to forgive, trust, and eventually love again. They are essential to the restoration process, but you've got to be willing to make a commitment to change. Your restoration will not end at the last page of this book; it's just the beginning.

You need to begin seeking God to not only reveal to you all the hidden damage that has been done within you, and begin to restore you, but also to lead you to where He would have you to be connected, for the spiritual parents that will help you on this journey, and if He's already placed you there, for the resolve to go the distance. Because God desires to restore you, but the question is *"Wilt thou be made whole?"* John 5:6 KJV

For assistance finding a church in you area contact us at
**word@newbirthkingdomchurch.org**

# ENDNOTES

1. Dr. Tim Clinton and Dr. Ron Hawkins, *Biblical Counseling Quick Reference Guide,* (Forest, VA: AACC Press, 2007)

# To Contact
# Pastor Tucker for
# Speaking Engagements:

⸏

**Mail:** Pastor Lewis L. Tucker Jr.

New Birth Kingdom Church

P.O. Box 10941

Lynchburg, VA 24506

**Phone:** 434-846-3030

**Email:** pastortuck@newbirthkingdomchurch.org

**Website:** www.newbirthkingdomchurch.org

Breinigsville, PA USA
23 March 2011
258215BV00001B/12/P

9 781432 728724